D1462711

101 Leadership Quotes

from

My Battlefield, Your Office

Leadership Lessons from the Front Lines

Justin Constantine

Lieutenant Colonel (ret), U.S. Marine Corps

ISBN-10: 0-9975783-0-0

ISBN-13: 978-0-9975783-0-0

Freeze Time Media

Cover illustration by Liz Pavlovic

INTRODUCTION

I joined the Marine Corps during my second year of law school and served as a criminal defense counsel and criminal prosecutor. But when I deployed to Iraq in 2006, it wasn't in the role of a JAG officer. In the Marine Corps all the officers learn the basics of many different jobs, so I volunteered for the deployment as a Civil Affairs Team Leader. I had the honor of leading a team of eight Marines and a Navy Corpsman, and we were attached to a Marine infantry battalion located halfway between Fallujah and Ramadi in Al-Anbar Province.

As a Civil Affairs officer, I was expected to develop contracts with the local population to help rebuild the basic infrastructure needed for any city. The projects were designed to provide clean running water, functioning electricity, driveable roads, and well-needed schools. Unfortunately, the fall of 2006 was an extremely volatile time for the Marine Corps in Iraq, and the insurgency there was at its most powerful level. Convincing the local Iraqis to work with us to rebuild the cities was virtually impossible when they would be visited at night by members of the insurgency with death threats for any indication of cooperation. That being said, I will always look back on the time I spent in Iraq as the highlight of my career—not too many other lawyers get to lead Marines in a war environment, and I learned a lot about myself, and effective leadership, while I was there.

I was out with a squad of Marines on a regular combat patrol on October 18, 2006, and we had just gotten to an area near one of our forward operating bases where we knew an enemy sniper was operating because he had already killed a few Marines. But, of course, that was not going to interfere with our mission.

We had a reporter with us that day, and I noticed at one of our stops that he was just standing around—a terrible idea if a sniper might be targeting you. When we got out of the vehicle at our next stop and started walking away from the Humvee, I said to him, "Hey Jay, you have to move faster here. Don't forget about the sniper. We don't want you to get hurt." Later, he told me that based on that, he took a big step forward.

A split second later, a bullet came in right where his head had been and hit the wall next to us. Before I could react, the next shot hit me behind my left ear and exited out my mouth, causing catastrophic damage along the way. In fact, the Marines around me thought that I had been killed, and when the Corpsman came running over, they told him, "Don't worry about the major—he's dead."

But Corpsman George Grant is an amazing young man, and even though blood was pouring out of my head and what was left of my face, George was able to focus on me and keeping me alive. Despite the sniper still shooting at us, and despite wearing 65 pounds of protective armor like we all did on our patrols, George proceeded to save my life. He somehow performed rescue breathing on my destroyed mouth, and then cut open my throat and performed an emergency tracheotomy on me so that I wouldn't drown on my own blood. In fact, George did such a perfect job on my tracheotomy that my plastic surgeon at the military hospital thought another surgeon had performed it.

Keep in mind that George was only 25 years old at the time. And keep in mind that George had never performed that kind of surgery on a human before—he had only done it once during a controlled training environment for Corpsmen at Camp Pendleton, California. He performed that surgery on a pig, and I don't know what that says about me, but the pig survived and so did I!

It is now 10 years since my injury, and I cannot see out of my left eye, I am missing most of my teeth and the end of my tongue, and I cannot talk perfectly clearly. I cannot run because the doctors removed several of the bones in my legs to use in reconstructing my upper and lower jaws. I also suffer from post-traumatic stress and a traumatic brain injury.

But you know what? Thanks to Navy Corpsman George Grant, my wife and family, and numerous individuals and organizations, I have had a very fortunate recovery. I retired as a lieutenant colonel, ultimately practiced law for 15 years, and now run my own business as an inspirational speaker and leadership advisor.

I have taken what I learned in the Marines and applied it to the corporate business world, because I learned that operating in the military and leading a team in the private or public sector have definite parallels. I know that most people do not have the benefit of learning leadership through an organization like the Marine Corps, but we can all benefit from the principles that our military holds dearly. This led me to write "My Battlefield, Your Office: Leadership Lessons from the Front Lines."

What you are reading now are 101 of the most poignant leadership quotes from "My Battlefield." Each quote comes from the heart and is based on my real life experience. Through my own reflective process, I collected the quotes I thought would be most impactful to those who take leadership seriously.

I can appreciate that sometimes in our hectic days we just have time to read one quick quote or focus on one idea. I hope that each one will give you something to think about and help you on your journey to be a better leader.

You can use this book however you want. You can read it from start to finish or flip through randomly. Perhaps you may want to journal about a particular quote, write a blog post, or simply meditate—I will leave that to you.

When you make a
command decision,
act swiftly using all
the intelligence at your
disposal.

Any successful business should be built on principles, but we are responsible for ourselves first. Your personal foundation transcends any place you work and allows you to use your talents in any position or company you may find yourself.

If you have integrity,
nothing else matters.
If you do not have
integrity, nothing else
matters.

No matter what you do, from working the streets of Fallujah to working the boardroom in New York, you should approach it with a long-range attitude, a focus on the future and on grand goals.

There is nothing more valuable in this day and age than a person who accomplishes what he says he will.

Never miss an
opportunity to pay
a compliment or
say you appreciate
something about
someone.

Being a leader is hard. Anyone who says otherwise has never been a true leader.

You need your staff to have the same vision and to desire to function with the same degree of integrity as you.

Having solid core principles is critical to personal and professional success.

Honorable actions are contagious. Inspire others by doing the right thing.

To define your vision realistically, you have to understand what drives your people, what their values are, and what they are capable of accomplishing with the right support and direction. You also need to have an intimate understanding of your corporate culture and the key characteristics of your business environment.

Leaders must always move forward, face danger and uncertainty, and take risks when there is no guarantee of success. Great leaders know that often the greatest danger is to do nothing in a world that is changing rapidly.

I know I will never be the Marine I once was. My career as a trial lawyer is over. I know that I will now, and for the rest of my life, have problems eating, drinking, speaking, and remembering things. I deal with those obstacles every day, but I still consider myself one of the luckiest people alive.

Understanding your people can only happen through close interaction with them.

Being a great leader means you are willing to take a hard look at yourself and identify your strengths and weaknesses.

We view leading Marines as a privilege – not a right or just some other job – and it is a privilege you have to earn every day. The same is true in the workplace.

Management and leadership is not hiding behind your desk and a closed door while handing out orders for employees to follow in emailed memos. It is about knowing your people and getting their feedback on what is and is not working. Leadership is being responsive to the needs of those who follow you and putting them in the best position to be successful in their jobs.

You cannot lead everybody the same way and realistically expect the same results – you often have to paint with a fine stroke, not a broad brush.

Be a man of principle. Fight for what you believe in. Keep your word. Live with integrity. Be brave. Believe in something bigger than yourself. Serve your country. Teach. Mentor. Give something back to society. Lead from the front. Conquer your fears. Be a good friend. Be humble and self-confident. Appreciate your friends and family. Be a leader and not a follower. Be valorous on the field of battle. And take responsibility for your actions.

– Major Doug Zembiec

When you are a leader and when your people are loyal to you and to each other, you can accomplish anything.

Marine leaders prioritize the accomplishment of the mission first, the welfare of their Marines second, and their own personal needs third.

Nobody will follow you if they do not feel you are willing to make the same sacrifice you are asking of them.

Everybody wants to know that they matter as a person and that they are not just some cog in the corporate machine. When a supervisor takes time to get to know them, the results are truly magical.

When you have the backing of those that work for you, it is so much easier to be successful.

Military battles talk about casualties, but every leader knows that each one of those casualties is a person and takes that to heart. As a leader in business, that is the same way to look at your employees. Profit, inventory, and anything else you measure are the results of the hard work of people – your people.

Remember what it felt like when a leader put your needs first – strive to regularly replicate that.

Don't use a checklist to get to know your people, but show your genuine interest in them and the rest will fall into place.

Developing effective teams is the single most important role of a leader.

Numbers and metrics do not determine leadership. Rather, leadership developing teamwork, trust, and the right attitude is how you get people to work toward those numbers and metrics. It is all about *people* – your people.

It is okay to ask for help and to lean on others for support.

Being a true leader often means doing things you do not want to do and taking actions you are not comfortable performing. Keep at the forefront of your mind that the goal of any leader is to reach the objectives of the organization.

A good leader does not put himself on a pedestal. He puts the men and women who report to him up on that stand.

What are your values? What do you stand for? Most importantly, if you ask other people around you, would they say your values are evident in how you deal with others?

Bad, ineffective
leadership looks
at people solely as
a resource to be
used up, rather than
nurtured.

A mature leader truly does have an open door policy.

I choose to embrace change. I want to live in the future, not the past. I am not defined by what happened to me, but how I have dealt with the change that has come along with it.

I have learned that through inner strength, humility, and a victorious spirit, we can each overcome the toughest obstacles.

Everybody needs
to row in the same
direction or you will
go around in circles.

When you make a mistake, take into account all of the factors that led to it, determine what you could have done differently and how you may have better utilized personnel, and think about how you can recognize a similar situation in the future.

Don't hold your people accountable for criteria outside their area of responsibility.

Good leadership means developing the talents of those working for you. When you go that extra step and act as a mentor, you are fulfilling one of your biggest responsibilities.

When your people receive a promotion, it should not be a threat or a source of fear to a good manager. Rather, one of the explicit goals of the manager's job should be making those for whom he is responsible shine in the organization.

Investing in your people not only increases productivity but also demonstrates that you care about them.

When my wife and I first identified that I had post-traumatic stress, it was difficult for me to wrap my head around that and to ask for the help that I needed.

When someone
identifies a fear
to you, recognize
the strength they
displayed in doing so.

Remember that there is only a razor's edge of difference between arrogance and self-confidence.

Many people who claim to be self-made success stories actually benefited from others in many different ways.

Having integrity of your own principles helps breed a consistent pattern of performance for your employees.

As a leader in your company, you need to know the difference between work and activity.

Relationships are critical to our well-being – make the time to invest in them.

America is full of opportunities for you to help others. We would be missing so much good if it were not for the millions of volunteers who participate in the organizations they support.

Let everyone know your vision and keep your staff and key players involved. Disseminate your vision far and wide. Take bold, decisive action when necessary. Synchronize your actions with your company's well-defined mission and purpose. Then, ultimately, your vision will become your reality.

Anyone who goes through any type of leadership training in the military learns that while meeting an objective is important, it is just as important to care for the personnel under you.

In the military, we are constantly taught to do our job, to do it well, and to determine how the simple act of doing our own job helps or could help those working next to us. Can you imagine how vibrant all of our companies would be if people took it upon themselves to adhere to that simple philosophy? Everyone in a leadership position can make that happen!

The most productive leaders are often those who regularly engage with their employees.

Never, never, never give up.

It does not take an architect to figure out that a house built on a firm foundation is going to weather storms better than one constructed on a beach. As individuals, we need something akin to that structural integrity at our core.

Those who perform at high levels are very clear about what they believe in, and those who perform at an average level are blurred as to their beliefs. The high performers will not compromise their values and principles; others will compromise for even the slightest advantage.

Not asking for help is counterproductive, shortsighted, and can adversely affect others.

Think for a minute how an environment valuing integrity could foster a better atmosphere at work. If you are a manager, it all starts with your integrity - sticking to your principles.

The best way to make
sure you are going
to be a success is to
make sure your team
is a success.

Most corporations want to promote people who do good work, maintain a positive attitude, and inspire their teams to improve their capabilities. So, although it may take time, keep on a steady and honorable course at work. That will pay huge dividends.

You can't have innovation, progress, or advancements without change.

By having a firm
set of principles, we
also do well when
we face indecision.

Whether you are the CEO of a Fortune 500 company, starting your own business, or working hard as a mid-level manager, you are there on the shoulders of others. It may have been teachers, family, employees, your current team, etc., but nobody gets to where he is alone.

Cherishing integrity and acting consistently is a great combination.

To develop your mission, but especially to communicate it with clarity, it is vital to ensure you can succinctly identify what the mission is. Succinct and clear identification of the mission will make it much more likely that others will buy into it.

All successful leaders take action and constantly drive their people and teams toward their vision. Once you identify the necessary steps you need to take and the resources you need to commit to achieve your vision – do it! Implement!

For the most part, leaders are made, not born. Even if born with innate leadership potential, that potential takes development and honing to be most effective. So, if you want to be an excellent leader, it is just like anything else: You have to study, learn, put your time in, and be seen as the person who gets the job done.

The moment you realize that you hold the solution to the very challenges you face is the moment your life changes. That realization puts you in control of your life. You are free to move forward, to overcome any obstacle in your path, and to create the life you really want.

Even the most successful person needs help at different points throughout life.

Only by identifying a strategic vision can you really determine long-term measurable goals.

Many managers and supervisors are promoted into their positions because they did a great job at a lower level. But they often have received no leadership training to help them expand their focus and scope of influence. Focusing on these new leaders is critical for a company's success.

In any discussion about leadership, we have to start with the premise that it is not just about effective management, but that a great leader puts his employees' needs first and empowers them to perform at their highest levels.

The most successful leaders know that they do not achieve their promotions in a vacuum. They are successful because they took seriously their position and responsibility as a leader, and they knew that meant responsibility for and to those under them. Great leaders know they are at the top of a pyramid and that they can only be there with the support of everyone beneath them.

Truly and consistently excellent companies do not function on a dictatorial basis. While final decisions are the responsibility of the people at the top of the hierarchical ladder, these leaders arrive at their conclusions only after listening to and evaluating the ideas of the people doing the actual work.

Officers
eat
last.

It is always helpful to remember what it feels like to do the work you are asking your employees to do.

As a leader, you cannot be afraid to ask others to start leading. One of your obligations as a manager is to help others get a taste of leadership and find out who has the strengths and abilities to lead.

True integrity does not have an on and off switch.

A proactive leader strives every day to get the team to work together and for each member to learn that they can depend on and trust each another.

Nothing in life remains constant. We are continually changing, adapting, and evolving. This is true in our personal as well as in our professional lives.

A poor leader says, "Woe is me. Why can't things be the way they always were?" A good leader says, "We are moving in a new direction now. This is exciting."

Being able to look at change for the opportunities it presents is an attitude. Just like any other leadership trait, it is something that someone can learn and hone with experience.

The essence of leadership is not the title or the trappings that may come with the position. It is the ability to successfully lead others to meet the desired goals and objectives.

Embrace change as I did. We can certainly feel sorry for ourselves momentarily when hit with some negative change in our life. But that negative could turn into something incredibly positive. Life is too long and filled with too many wonderful events to focus solely on the negative. If you are a leader in business, in your community, or in your family, many opportunities are heading your way. Some of them may be disguised as an unwanted change.

If your talents have propelled you to a successful point of leadership in business, please use those same gifts to help your community and your country. That is how America became the great country she is today. It is going to take the continued efforts of people with concern, vision, and leadership to help our towns, states, and country continue to grow and be the land of opportunity we still believe the United States to be.

Take responsibility for your actions.

It is important
that a good leader
learn from his
mistakes.

Remaining focused on your vision and continuing to put forth the effort to reach it – one step at a time – is what separates life's great achievers from those who merely dream but never act.

A good leader must know the strengths and weaknesses of everyone on his staff. A great leader will help a staff member work on those weaknesses.

Developing
your team is a
continuous effort
that requires
constant attention.

It is a good idea to write down your principles for work and for life in general. I hope they are the same for both. Writing your principles down makes them real, concrete, and something you can refer back to when things get tough. Your list of principles is always a work in progress. However, having the integrity to stick to your principles will be your key to succeed in business over the long run.

A simple pat on the back and saying "good job" to one of your people will sometimes have more influence than any pay raise or formal award ceremony. If you have worked hard to build your team, if they look up to you, then your simple recognition and encouragement will take your group to the heights you want to reach.

Truly responsible leaders do not make excuses when things go wrong. Good leaders do not blame others. They save their energy, deal, and focus on the future. Leaders stay calm, cool, and collected. Leaders think about what to do, not what has happened. They focus on the opportunities of tomorrow rather than the problems or accolades of yesterday.

As a leader, developing your vision, clearly articulating it, and then disseminating it through a number of different channels is critical.

When you do not constantly move toward your vision, you let others shape your destiny.

Even in America, so many people need help with the most basic aspects of life. Volunteering is a great way to help others who are not as fortunate as you.

Leaders who comprehend that they will have to deal with all types of change, and are prepared to be effective when it happens, will go far. An even better leader, though, will study what is going on around her and anticipate the change to take advantage of it.

A leader can come from any background if she has the desire to make a difference.

You cannot stop change from happening, but you can embrace it and prepare for it.

Made in the USA
Columbia, SC
12 September 2017